Vegetarian

Recipes from Around the World

Sue Townsend and Caroline Young

Heinemann
LIBRARY

www.heinemann.co.uk/library

Visit our website to find out more information about **Heinemann Library** books.

To order:
- ☎ Phone 44 (0) 1865 888066
- 🖹 Send a fax to 44 (0) 1865 314091
- 💻 Visit the Heinemann Bookshop at www.heinemann.co.uk/library to browse our catalogue and order online.

First published in Great Britain by Heinemann Library, Halley Court, Jordan Hill, Oxford OX2 8EJ, part of Harcourt Education.

Heinemann is a registered trademark of Harcourt Education Ltd.

Editorial: Nancy Dickmann, Andrew Solway and Jennifer Tubbs
Design: Jo Hinton-Malivoire and Tinstar Design Limited (www.tinstar.co.uk)
Illustrations: Nicholas Beresford-Davies
Picture Research: Catherine Bevan
Production: Séverine Ribierre

Originated by Dot Gradations Ltd
Printed in China
by Wing King Tong

ISBN 0 431 11730 6
07 06 05 04 03
10 9 8 7 6 5 4 3 2 1

British Library Cataloguing in Publication Data
Townsend, Sue & Young, Caroline
Vegetarian. – (A World of Recipes)
641.5'123
A full catalogue record for this book is available from the British Library.

Acknowledgements
The publishers would like to thank the following for permission to reproduce photographs: Corbis: p. 6; Gareth Boden: all other photographs.

Cover photographs reproduced with permission of Gareth Boden.

Every effort has been made to contact copyright holders of any material reproduced in this book. Any omissions will be rectified in subsequent printings if notice is given to the publishers.

Contents

Key

* easy

** medium

*** difficult

Words appearing in the text in bold, **like this**, are explained in the glossary.

Vegetarian food

Many people in the world are **vegetarian**. This means that they do not eat any meat. Some vegetarians eat fish, but no meat. Other vegetarians, called **vegans**, do not eat any food that has come from an animal, including milk and eggs. Instead of dairy products, they may eat foods made with soya milk, from soya beans. Whatever people eat, it is important to make sure that their body is getting the **nutrients** it needs.

Is it healthy to be a vegetarian?

Animal foods, such as meat, fish and eggs, contain **protein**, which our bodies need to stay healthy. Fruit, **pulses** and vegetables do not have as much protein as animal foods, but eating a good range of them will give you all the protein you need. Here are some examples:

squash

cabbage

pineapple

swede

peas

lemon

red peppers

potatoes

sweetcorn

yoghurt

carrots

apples

onion

turnips

garlic

pecans

ginger

bread

cheese

beans

leeks

cinnamon

Pulses

Pulses are beans and seeds from plants. They include broad beans, black-eyed beans and chick peas. Pulses are a very good source of protein and can be cooked in many different ways. You can buy most pulses dried or tinned.

Nuts

Nuts, such as walnuts, pecan nuts and peanuts, are another good source of protein. Many cooking styles around the world use nuts in sweet and savoury recipes. Nuts contain quite a lot of fat, so do not eat too many.

Dairy or soya products

Milk, cheese and yoghurt are dairy products. They contain protein and **calcium**, which help to give us strong bones and teeth. Vegans can get calcium from dairy substitutes, such as soya milk with added calcium. Supermarkets sell both types of products.

Fruit and vegetables

Fruit and vegetables are a good source of **vitamins**, which everyone needs to stay healthy. You can buy many different kinds of fruit and vegetables in supermarkets and grocery shops. They come from all over the world. Dried fruit, and canned and frozen fruit and vegetables, contain nutrients, too.

Cereals

More people in the world eat rice every day than any other food. It is a **staple** ingredient in many countries. People also eat other cereals, such as wheat and barley. Health food shops sell a variety of grains, including bulgur wheat.

Around the world

There are more **vegetarians** today than there have ever been, and their numbers are growing. There are several reasons why people choose not to eat meat.

Why are people vegetarian?

In poorer parts of the world, people may have no choice about being vegetarian. Meat is a luxury food that they cannot afford. Some families keep a cow, goat or chicken for their milk or their eggs, but their animal is too valuable to kill for meat.

Many millions of people avoid eating meat for religious reasons. The followers of Hinduism and Buddhism, for example, believe that they should respect all living beings and live in a way that does not cause any harm. Because of this, many are vegetarians.

▶ *A wide variety of vegetables are being sold at this market stall in India.*

Other vegetarians have made a choice not to eat meat. They believe that it is wrong to breed and kill other living things for our food. Many people feel that they will enjoy better health if they follow a vegetarian diet, so they do not eat meat.

The vegetarian world

There are vegetarians in every part of the world. The recipes in this book come from all around the world. The map below shows you where the countries which the recipes come from, are located.

Before you start

Kitchen rules

There are a few basic rules you should always follow when you are cooking:

- Ask an adult if you can use the kitchen.
- Some cooking processes, especially those involving hot water or oil, can be dangerous. When you see this sign, take extra care or ask an adult to help.
- Wash your hands before you start.
- Wear an apron to protect your clothes.
- Be very careful when you use sharp knives.
- Never leave pan handles sticking out, in case you knock them.
- Always use oven gloves to lift things in and out of the oven.
- Wash fruit and vegetables before you use them.
- Always wash chopping boards very well after use, especially after chopping raw meat, fish or poultry.
- Use a separate chopping board for onions and garlic, if possible.

How long will it take?

Some of these recipes are quick and easy, and some are more difficult and take longer. The strip across the right-hand side of each recipe page tells you how long it takes to prepare a dish from start to finish. It also shows how difficult it is to make: each recipe is * (easy), ** (medium) or *** (difficult).

Quantities and measurements

You can see how many people each recipe will serve at the top of each right-hand page. You can multiply or divide the quantities if you want to cook for more or fewer people.

Ingredients for recipes can be measured in two different ways. Metric measurements use grams and millilitres. Imperial measurements use ounces and fluid ounces. This book uses metric measurements. If you want to convert these into imperial measurements, see the chart on page 44.

In the recipes, you will see the following abbreviations:

tbsp = tablespoon   g = grams   cm = centimetres

tsp = teaspoon   ml = millilitres

Utensils

To cook the recipes in this book, you will need these utensils (as well as essentials, such as spoons, plates and bowls):

- plastic or glass chopping board (easier to clean than wooden ones)
- food processor or blender
- large frying pan
- 20 cm heavy-based non-stick frying pan
- measuring jug
- sieve
- small and large saucepans, with lids
- set of scales
- sharp knife
- slotted spoon
- kitchen spatula
- baking sheets
- lemon squeezer
- potato masher
- apple corer
- whisk
- 18 cm plate
- pastry brush.

 Whenever you use kitchen knives, be very careful.

Broad bean pâté with ciabatta toast (Italy)

There are many **vegetarian** recipes from Italy. This one is from Tuscany, an area famous both for its old towns and cities, and for its beautiful countryside. This recipe uses frozen broad beans, because fresh ones are only available for a short time each year. Ciabatta (pronounced *chee-a-batta*) is a type of Italian bread, which you can find in many supermarkets or bakeries. Serve the pâté with some salad as an ideal starter, light lunch or snack.

What you need

1 onion
3 garlic cloves
2 tbsp olive oil
400 g frozen broad beans
70 g reduced-fat
   cream cheese
1 lemon
1 ciabatta loaf

What you do

1 **Peel** and finely **chop** the onion and garlic.

(!) 2 Heat the oil in a small frying pan over a medium heat. **Fry** the onion and garlic for 5 minutes, until they are softened. Leave them to cool.

(!) 3 Put the frozen broad beans into a saucepan and cover them with water. Bring the water to the **boil**, **cover** the pan and **simmer** the beans for 5 minutes.

4 **Drain** the beans and let them cool down.

5 Put them into a food processor or blender. Add the cream cheese and the fried onion mixture.

6 Cut the lemon in half. Using a lemon squeezer, squeeze the juice from both halves.

7 Add the lemon juice to the bean mixture, and **blend** until smooth.

8 Using a spatula, scrape the pâté into a bowl for serving.

9 Cut the ciabatta into 2 cm thick slices. Heat a grill and **toast** the slices of bread on each side, until lightly browned.

10 Serve the ciabatta warm with the pâté and some salad.

11

Walnut, fenugreek and yoghurt soup (Iran)

For hundreds of years, Iran was in the middle of trading routes between Europe and Asia. Iran's cooking style has been influenced by the many different people who have visited the country throughout history. In Iran, this soup is served hot or cold, as a starter or light lunch. It contains the **ground** seeds of a plant called fenugreek. Fenugreek leaves can be added to salads, too.

What you need

1 onion
1 tbsp vegetable oil
   or butter
50 g walnuts
1 tsp ground
   fenugreek
600 ml water
1 tbsp cornflour
500 ml natural
   yoghurt

What you do

1 **Peel** and finely **chop** the onion.

2 Heat the oil or butter in a saucepan over a medium heat. Add the onion and **fry** over a medium to low heat for 4–5 minutes, until it has softened.

3 Put the walnuts into a blender, and **blend** until finely chopped. Add the walnuts and fenugreek to the saucepan.

4 In a bowl, stir 4 tbsp of the water into the cornflour.

5 Add the rest of the water to the pan. **Cover** and **simmer** for 20 minutes, and then allow to cool for 5 minutes.

6 Stir the yoghurt into the cornflour mixture. Add 240 ml of the liquid from the saucepan to the yoghurt mixture, and stir well.

7 Slowly pour the yoghurt mixture into the pan, stirring all the time. Reheat the soup, but do not let it **boil.** Serve hot or cold with some bread.

MAKING YOGHURT

To make your own yoghurt, heat 500 ml of milk until it is just boiling. Let it cool until it is warm, then stir in 2 tbsp plain natural yoghurt. Pour into a clean jar and keep in a warm place for 6–8 hours, until set. **Chill** the yoghurt for 12 hours before serving.

13

Black-eyed bean cakes (Ethiopia)

Farmers in north and central African countries, such as Ethiopia, grow black-eyed beans, or black-eyed peas, as they are sometimes called. African cooks usually soak the beans, pour them into a bowl and **mash** them with a simple stone or wooden tool. They **deep-fry** their bean cakes, but this version fries them in a little oil.

What you need

200 g dried black-
   eyed beans
150 g sweet potato
1 onion
pinch of salt
half a red chilli (if
   you like them)
1 tbsp flour
3 tbsp oil

What you do

1 Put the black-eyed beans into a bowl, and cover them with cold water. Leave them to soak overnight.

2 **Drain** the beans. Rub them between your hands so that the skins loosen. Put them into a bowl and cover them with water. Tip the water and skins away.

3 **Peel** the sweet potato and cut it into 2 cm chunks. Peel and finely **chop** the onion.

4 Put the potato into a saucepan, cover it with **boiling** water and add a pinch of salt. Cook for 15 minutes, or until it is tender, and then drain it.

5 Cut the half a chilli in half lengthways and throw away the seeds. Chop the chilli finely. Wash your hands thoroughly after handling chilli. The juice can make your eyes and skin very sore.

6 Put the beans into a blender. Add the onion and chilli, and **blend** until smooth. Add the potato and blend again.

7 Sprinkle a little of the flour on to a work surface. Take out 2 tbsp of the mixture, and shape it into a ball. Then flatten it into a fritter shape. Do this with the rest of the mixture, to make about 20 fritters.

(!) 8 Heat the oil in a large frying pan over a medium heat. **Fry** the bean cakes, four or five at a time, for 4 minutes on each side, until golden. Lift the cooked bean cakes on to kitchen paper.

9 Serve straightaway, with cooked, green vegetables or salad, as a starter or light lunch.

Gobi paratha (India)

Many people in India are **vegetarian**. They cook different dishes using vegetables and **pulses**. In India, people often scoop up their food with flat breads, such as parathas. This recipe is for a paratha stuffed with vegetables. Parathas can also be flavoured with spices or fried onion.

What you need

100 g cauliflower florets
1 tsp salt
1 onion
quarter of a green chilli
  (if you like them)
2.5 cm piece fresh ginger
1 tbsp fresh coriander
  (chopped)
300 g wholewheat flour
4 tbsp ghee (clarified
  butter)
  or vegetable oil

What you do

1 **Chop** or **grate** the cauliflower florets finely, into very small pieces. Tip them into a sieve over the sink. Sprinkle them with some salt, and leave to **drain** for 30 minutes.

2 Meanwhile, **peel** and finely chop the onion.

3 Cut the piece of chilli in half, and throw away the seeds. Chop the chilli finely. Wash your hands thoroughly after touching raw chilli.

4 Peel and grate the ginger. Rinse the cauliflower pieces and pat them dry.

5 Put the cauliflower, onion, chilli, ginger and coriander into a bowl, and stir well.

6 Put the flour into a bowl, add 2 tbsp ghee or vegetable oil, and a pinch of salt. Stir in 200 ml water. Using your hands, make the mixture into a stiff dough.

7 Sprinkle a little flour on a work surface. Stretch the dough, fold it over, then press it with the palm of your hand. Turn in round by one quarter, and repeat. **Knead** it in this way for 3 minutes.

8 Cut the dough into four pieces. Using a rolling pin, roll each one out to form a 15 cm circle. Brush a little ghee or oil over each.

9 Scatter the cauliflower mixture over the circles. Gather each circle up to make a ball. Carefully roll each ball out into a 22 cm circle.

⚠ 10 Brush each paratha with a little ghee or oil. Heat a heavy-based frying pan over a medium heat. **Fry** each paratha for 3–4 minutes on each side, until golden brown.

11 Serve warm with a vegetable curry (see page 36), **chutney** and rice.

Barley and vegetable soup (Poland)

Winters in Poland can be extremely cold, so warm, filling soups such as this one are a popular lunch or supper dish. Polish farmers grow the vegetables this soup contains, as well as many different kinds of fruit. They bottle fruit or make it into jam, before **exporting** it to other countries.

What you need

75 g pearl barley
1.5 litres hot water
1 carrot
1 parsnip
2 potatoes
1 celery stick
2 onions
2 tbsp vegetable oil
50 g button mushrooms
2 vegetable stock cubes
salt and pepper

What you do

1 Put the pearl barley into a bowl and cover it with cold water. Leave it to soak for 4 hours.

(!) 2 Drain the barley. Put it into a pan, add half the hot water and bring it to the **boil. Cover** the pan and **simmer** for 30 minutes.

3 Peel the carrot and parsnip, and trim off both ends. Peel the potatoes.

4 Cut all three vegetables into 1 cm slices, and then into cubes.

5 Trim the ends off the celery. Cut it into 1 cm slices.

6 Peel and **chop** the onions.

18

(!) 7 Heat the oil in a large saucepan over a medium heat. **Fry** the onion for 3 minutes, or it is until softened. Add the celery, potato, carrot and parsnip. Stir well and cook for 5 minutes, stirring occasionally.

8 **Slice** the mushrooms thinly and add them to the pan.

(!) 9 Add the pearl barley and the liquid it cooked in. Pour in the rest of the hot water.

10 Crumble the stock cubes into the pan, stirring well. Bring to the boil, **cover** and simmer for 20 minutes.

11 Add a pinch of salt and pepper. Spoon the soup into bowls. Serve with crusty bread.

Chick peas with sugar snap peas (Senegal)

Many traditional African dishes are made in one pot, hung over a fire. All the ingredients are cooked together as a complete meal, as in this recipe from Senegal, in north-west Africa. Sugar snap peas are grown throughout Africa.

What you need

1 onion
1 garlic clove
450 g sugar snap peas
2 tomatoes
1 tbsp vegetable oil
1 tsp black mustard seeds
1 tsp **ground** cumin
400 g can chick peas

What you do

1 **Peel** and finely **chop** the onion and garlic.

2 Cut the ends off the sugar snap peas and cut them in half.

3 Chop the tomatoes.

4 Heat the oil in a medium saucepan over a medium heat. Add the onion and garlic, and **fry** for 3 minutes, or until they are softened.

5 Stir in the sugar snap peas and tomatoes and cook for 5 minutes.

6 Add the mustard seeds and cumin, and cook for 1 minute.

7 Empty the chick peas into a sieve. Rinse them under running cold water.

8 Stir the chick peas into the sugar snap peas mixture. **Cover** the pan and cook for 4–5 minutes, until piping hot.

9 Spoon on to a serving dish. Serve straight away.

Colcannon (Ireland)

For centuries, potatoes were a **staple** food in Ireland. If the potato harvest failed, many people starved. Colcannon is a traditional dish that mixes potatoes with spring onions and cabbage. If it is served at Halloween, a silver coin or charm is sometimes stirred into the mixture – whoever gets the charm is supposed to marry within a year.

What you need

750 g potatoes
pinch of salt
half a bunch of
   spring onions
100 g cabbage
100 ml milk
50 g butter

What you do

1 **Peel** the potatoes and cut them into 4 cm chunks. Put them into a pan with a pinch of salt.

2 Cover the potatoes with **boiling** water. Bring the water back to the boil, **cover** and **simmer** for 17 minutes (you may need to set a timer for this).

3 Trim the ends off the spring onions and throw them away. Cut the spring onions into thin **slices**.

4 Wash the cabbage and **chop** it into small pieces.

5 Add the onions and the cabbage to the potatoes in the pan, and cook for a further 3 minutes.

6 Carefully **drain** the potatoes, onions and cabbage into a colander, and then put them back into the hot pan.

7 **Mash** the vegetables with a potato masher. Add enough milk to make a light, fluffy mixture.

8 Stir in half the butter, and some salt and pepper.

9 Put the Colcannon into a serving dish. Make several dips in the top with a teaspoon and put a little bit of the rest of the butter into each dip. Serve hot, with other vegetables.

23

Olive, pomegranate and walnut salad (Turkey)

Summers are very hot in Turkey, so people there usually eat a light lunch. They eat their main meal in the evening, when it is cooler. This recipe is from south-eastern Turkey, where farmers grow all the ingredients – olives, walnuts and pomegranates.

What you need

1 pomegranate
50 g fresh coriander
1 bunch spring onions
120 g walnuts
25 g fresh sorrel or
   spinach leaves
120 g Queen green
   olives

*For the **dressing:***
3 tbsp olive oil
1½ tbsp lemon juice
salt and pepper

What you do

1 Cut the pomegranate in half. Hold each half skin-side up over a bowl, and tap it with a rolling pin so that the seeds drop into the bowl.

2 **Chop** the coriander finely.

3 Trim the ends off the spring onions and throw them away. Cut the spring onions into thin **slices**.

4 Put the walnuts into a blender and **blend** until roughly chopped.

5 Rinse the sorrel or spinach leaves under running cold water, and pat them dry with a clean tea towel. Cut off the tough stalks.

6 Put all the dressing ingredients into a small screw-topped jar.

7 Shake all the salad ingredients together in a bowl. Shake the dressing well, pour it over the salad and toss again.

8 Spoon the salad on to individual plates, and serve with crusty bread.

OLIVES
Olives grow on trees in groups called groves. Some olive trees can produce olives for up to 300 years. The olives are harvested and soaked in salt water for eating, or crushed to make olive oil.

Sweetcorn, pepper and pumpkin stew (Venezuela)

Cooking all the ingredients for a meal in the same pot is part of traditional cooking in Venezuela, South America. Serve this vegetable stew as a main meal with crusty bread or rice.

What you need

2 onions
1 garlic clove
400 g pumpkin or
  butternut squash
2 corns on the cob,
 thawed if frozen
4 tomatoes
1 red pepper
4 small–medium potatoes
2 tbsp vegetable oil
100 g peas, fresh or frozen
1 tbsp fresh
  chopped marjoram

What you do

1 **Peel** and finely **chop** the onions and garlic.

2 Peel the pumpkin or butternut squash, throw away the seeds and cut the flesh into 2 cm chunks.

3 If using fresh corns on the cob, pull the leaves and silky threads off.

4 Cut the tomatoes into quarters. Cut the pepper in half, and throw away the stalk and seeds. Cut the flesh into 3 cm pieces.

5 Peel the potatoes and cut them into 2 cm chunks.

(!) 6 Heat the oil in a flameproof casserole dish or large pan over a medium heat. **Fry** the onion for 3 minutes, add the garlic and fry for 1 minute more.

7 Add the rest of the prepared vegetables, marjoram, salt and pepper and 450 ml of water to the pan. **Cover** and **simmer** for 25–30 minutes.

8 Using a slotted spoon, lift the sweetcorn on to a board. When it is cool, cut it into 1 cm thick slices.

9 Add the sweetcorn and peas to the pan, and cook for 5 minutes.

10 Stir the stew, and spoon it into a serving dish (if you cooked it in a pan). Serve hot.

Tabbouleh (Lebanon)

Lebanon is in the Middle East, between Israel and Syria. Tabbouleh is a traditional Lebanese recipe, but people all over the Middle East make it. They may change some of the ingredients, depending on what is available locally, but it always includes bulgur wheat. Serve it with **pitta bread** or with other dishes, as a side salad.

What you need

175 g bulgur (or cracked) wheat
1 lemon
2 tbsp olive oil
quarter of a cucumber
2 spring onions
6 cherry tomatoes
4 tbsp chopped fresh parsley
2 tbsp chopped fresh mint

What you do

1 Put the bulgur wheat into a heatproof bowl. Pick out any small stones.

(!) 2 Pour 550 ml **boiling** water over the wheat and stir well. Leave it for 30 minutes, stirring from time to time.

3 Put a sieve over the sink and **drain** the wheat.

4 Cut the lemon in half. Using a lemon squeezer, squeeze the juice from both halves.

5 Stir the lemon juice and olive oil into the bulgur wheat.

6 Cut the cucumber into long slices 1 cm thick, then cut each slice into strips 1 cm thick. Cut across each strip to make 1 cm cubes.

7 Trim the ends off the spring onions. Cut the spring onions into ½ cm slices.

8 Cut the cherry tomatoes in half. Stir the chopped herbs and tomatoes into the bulgur wheat with the cucumber. Add some salt and pepper.

9 Serve straightaway, with pitta bread or crusty bread, or keep it in the fridge (it will keep for up to 2 days).

Winter vegetable goulash (Hungary)

In Hungary, winters are very cold and few things grow. Hungarians store vegetables in a dry, dark place, and cook them with tomatoes and a mild, red spice, paprika, to make this stew, called goulash. Goulash can also have beans or meat as its main ingredient. Serve it as a main dish, with rice, pasta or crusty bread.

What you need

2 onions
2 carrots
2 parsnips
200 g swede
100 g turnip
   (if you like it)
2 tbsp vegetable oil
1 tbsp paprika
2 tbsp plain flour
8 small new potatoes
400 g can chopped
   tomatoes
1 vegetable stock cube
2 tsp cornflour
142 ml pot soured cream

*To **garnish**:*
2 tbsp chopped
   fresh parsley

What you do

1 **Peel** and finely **chop** the onions.

2 Peel and **slice** the carrots and parsnips.

3 Peel the swede and turnip (if using). Cut them into 2 cm thick slices, then into 2 cm chunks.

(!)4 Heat the oil in a large saucepan. Add the onions and **fry** them for 3 minutes, until softened.

5 Stir in the chopped-up vegetables and paprika, and cook for 5 minutes, stirring from time to time.

6 Sprinkle the flour over the vegetables and cook for 1 minute, stirring all the time.

(!)7 Pour 300 ml of **boiling** water over the vegetables. Add the new potatoes and canned tomatoes.

8 Crumble the stock cube over the pan and stir well. **Cover** and **simmer** for 25 minutes.

9 In a cup, mix the cornflour with 2 tbsp cold water. Stir the mixture into the soured cream, and then stir the cream into the vegetable mixture.

10 Carefully spoon the hot goulash into a serving dish, and sprinkle with parsley to serve.

Cheese fondue (Switzerland)

Sharing a fondue with friends is a popular Swiss tradition. Everyone takes turns to dip cubes of bread or vegetables into melted cheese in a fondue pan. A small burner under the pan keeps the cheese warm. If you do not have a **fondue set**, gently warm the ingredients in a heavy-based pan over a low heat on the hob. Keep the mixture warm by placing the pan over a heated dish-warmer.

What you need

200 ml grape juice
1 tsp cornflour
1 garlic clove
200 g Gruyère cheese
200 g Emmenthal cheese
1 French loaf (baguette)
4 thick slices rye bread
1 apple
2 tbsp lemon juice
2 carrots

What you do

1 Mix 2 tbsp of the grape juice with the cornflour to make a smooth paste.

2 **Peel** and crush the garlic. Put it into the fondue pan with the cornflour mixture and the rest of the grape juice. Stir well.

3 Cut the rind off both the cheeses. Cut each piece into 1 cm thick slices, then 1 cm wide strips. Now cut the strips into 1 cm cubes.

4 **Slice** the baguette into 2.5 cm slices, then cut each slice into quarters. Cut the rye bread into 3 cm cubes.

5 Cut the apple into eight wedges. Cut out the core and throw it away. Cut the wedges into 2 cm chunks. Put them in a bowl with the lemon juice.

6 Peel the carrots and cut them into 3 cm chunks.

⚠ 7 Ask an adult to light the fondue burner. Put the pan on top and let the mixture warm, but not **boil**. Add the cheese, stirring until melted.

8 Drain the lemon juice from the apple. Put the apple, bread and carrots on to plates.

9 Give each person a fork (a long fondue fork, if you have them).

10 Each person, in turn, puts a piece of bread, apple or carrot on their fork, dips it into the cheese, stirs the mixture once, takes the fork out and eats! (Take care: the melted cheese will be very hot.)

Vegetable Cornish pasties (England)

Cornwall is in the far south-west of England. These filled pastry envelopes, called pasties, were first made as lunch for miners working deep in the Cornish tin-mines. The men could not wash their hands before eating, so they held a pastry corner as they ate, then threw away the dirty bit. They are ideal as part of a picnic or as a lunch.

What you need

125 g potatoes
125 g carrots
125 g swede
half a vegetable
   stock cube
1 onion
1 tbsp vegetable oil
1 tbsp flour
500 g packet ready-
   made shortcrust
   pastry
1 egg

To *garnish:*
sprigs of fresh parsley

What you do

1 Peel the potatoes, carrots and swede. Cut each into 1 cm slices, then into 1 cm cubes. Put these vegetables into a saucepan, and crumble in half a stock cube.

(!) 2 Cover the vegetables with **boiling** water, bring back to the boil and cook for 10 minutes.

(!) 3 Peel and finely **chop** the onion. Heat the oil in a small pan, and **fry** the onion over a low to medium heat for 4 minutes.

(!) 4 Drain the potato, swede and carrots, and then add them to the onion. Leave them to cool completely.

5 Preheat the oven to gas mark 6/220 °C/400 °F. Sprinkle the flour on to a work surface. Use a rolling pin to roll the pastry out until it is about 3 mm thick.

6 Put an 18 cm plate on the pastry and cut around it. Repeat this to make six pastry circles.

7 Spoon the vegetables along the centre of each circle. Keep them away from the edge.

8 Brush a little water around the circles' edges. Fold the pastry over the filling. Press the pastry edge between your fingers to make a zig-zag ridge along the edge of each pasty.

9 Put the pasties on a baking tray. **Beat** the egg and brush a little over each pasty.

10 **Bake** for 25 minutes, until golden. Let the pasties cool a little before eating them, garnished with a sprig of parsley.

Pineapple curry (Sri Lanka)

Sri Lanka is an island in the Indian Ocean, just off the southern tip of India. This recipe uses pineapples and coconuts, two of the island's main crops. It also uses the dried leaves of the curry plant, which add a spicy flavour. Use a heavy-based saucepan for this recipe, if you can. Sri Lankan cooks use a pot called a '*chatty*'.

What you need

quarter of a fresh chilli
  (if you like it)
1 tsp mustard seeds
1 shallot
1 large, ripe pineapple
quarter of a stem of
  lemon grass
1 tbsp vegetable oil
3 dried curry leaves
100 ml coconut milk
pinch of saffron
1 small cinnamon stick
½ tsp **ground** cumin

What you do

1 **Chop** the quarter chilli finely (if you are using it), and then wash your hands thoroughly. Chilli juice can make your eyes and skin very sore.

2 Put the mustard seeds into a small frying pan, and **dry-fry** them over a medium heat for 30 seconds, until they 'pop'. Tip them on to a plate.

3 **Peel** and finely chop the shallot.

4 Cut the pineapple in half. Cut off the thick skin and leaves, and throw them away. Cut out the tough core in the middle, and throw it away. Chop the flesh into 2 cm chunks.

5 Peel off the outer leaves off the lemon grass. Trim off the root end and throw it away. Finely chop the lemon grass.

(!) 6 Heat the oil in a saucepan over a medium heat. **Fry** the shallot for 1 minute. Add the lemon grass and curry leaves, and fry for 1 minute.

7 Stir in the coconut milk and all the other ingredients, except the ground cumin. **Simmer** for 10 minutes, stirring from time to time.

8 Stir in the cumin, and simmer for 5 minutes. Take the cinnamon out, and serve hot, with rice.

Pecan pie (USA)

Pecan nuts are an important crop for farmers in the southern USA. They **export** them all over the world. Pecan nuts have a sweeter flavour than most nuts. Pecan pie is a popular traditional dish all over the USA. It is delicious warm or cold.

What you need

50 g dark soft brown sugar
4 tbsp golden syrup
1 tbsp butter
18 cm shortcrust pastry
  flan case
200 g pecan halves
1 egg
1 tsp vanilla essence

What you do

1 Put the sugar, golden syrup and butter into a pan. Heat them very gently over a low heat until the butter has melted. Stir well and leave to cool.

2 **Preheat** the oven to gas mark 4/180 °C/350 °F.

3 Put the pastry case on to a baking sheet.

4 Scatter half the pecans over the pastry, and level them. Arrange a circle of pecan halves around the edge of the pastry, and then another circle inside it. Keep making circles of nuts until you reach the centre.

5 **Beat** the egg and the vanilla essence with a fork. Stir this into the cooled sugar mixture, and then pour the liquid over the pecan nuts.

6 **Bake** the pie for 30 minutes, or until the egg and sugar mixture has set in the centre of the pie. Cool for 15 minutes.

7 Cut the pie into six slices, and serve with ice cream or cream.

THE HISTORY OF PECAN PIE

In the late seventeenth century, French explorers settled in New Orleans, USA. The Native Americans living there introduced them to the pecan nut. The French settlers invented Pecan pie – a delicious way to enjoy the nuts.

Apple pancakes (the Netherlands)

People in the Netherlands enjoy sweet and savoury pancakes. They might cook them with cheese, ham or fruit. Traditionally, Dutch cooks do not roll their pancakes up around the filling. Instead, they cook the filling with the batter, and serve the pancake flat on a large plate. This recipe is a particularly popular one in the Netherlands.

What you need

100 g plain flour
2 tsp soft brown sugar
1 tsp **ground** cinnamon
¼ tsp ground cloves
1 egg
200 ml milk
1 red apple
1 green apple
4 tsp vegetable oil

What you do

1 Sift the flour, sugar and ground spices into a bowl. Using your fingers, make a dip in the middle.

2 Beat the egg, add the milk and beat until well mixed. Pour the mixture into the dip in the flour, and gradually stir the liquid into the flour.

3 Beat the pancake batter well, and then put it on one side. Turn the oven on to its lowest setting.

4 Use an apple corer to take the apples' cores out.

5 Cut the apples in half, and then into thin **slices**. Stir the apple slices into the batter.

(!) 6 Heat ½ tsp oil in an 18 cm frying pan. Using a metal tablespoon, add 2 tablespoons of pancake batter and apple slices to the pan. Tilt the pan to cover the bottom with batter.

7 Cook for 2–3 minutes over a low to medium heat, until the pancake is golden brown on one side.

8 Use a fish slice to flip the pancake over, and cook the other side. Lift the pancake on to a plate, put another plate on top, and keep it warm in the oven while you cook the rest of the batter in the same way.

9 Serve the pancakes hot, either on their own, or with a little golden syrup or ice cream.

Athol brosse (Scotland)

Athol brosse means 'broth, or thick soup, from Athol', which is an area in Scotland. The main ingredients are all produced in Scotland – oatmeal, honey and raspberries. If you prefer, replace the cream with soya cream. Serve as a dessert, or as a cool treat on a hot day.

What you need

6 tbsp pinhead oatmeal
450 ml double cream
3 tbsp runny honey
200 g fresh raspberries
sprigs of mint

What you do

1 Scatter the oatmeal on to a baking tray.

2 Heat the grill to medium. Put the baking tray under the grill, and **grill** the oatmeal for about 1 minute, until the oatmeal starts to turn golden brown. Set it aside to cool.

3 Put the cream into a bowl. Using a hand-held electric whisk or balloon whisk, **whisk** the cream until it starts becoming firmer.

4 Spoon the honey over the cream.

5 Tip the oatmeal into the cream. Using a metal spoon, cut through the cream to **fold** it in.

6 Keeping four raspberries aside, divide the rest up into four glass bowls. Spoon the cream mixture on top of the raspberries.

7 Top each glass with a raspberry and a sprig of fresh mint.

8 **Chill** for 30 minutes before serving.

HEATHERY HONEY

Bees collect pollen from flowers to make into honey. The bees that make Scottish honey have gathered pollen from the heather that covers the hills and mountains of Scotland. Scots say that this makes their honey taste unlike any other kind.

Further information

Here are some places to find out more about vegetarian food and cooking.

Books

Kids Can Cook: Vegetarian Recipes, Dorothy Bates (Book Publishing Company, 2000)
Vegetarian Cooking Around the World, Alison Behnke (Lerner Publishing Company, 2002)
Vegetarian Cooking for Beginners, Fiona Watts (Usborne, 1999)

Websites

www.bbc.co.uk/food/children/feature_vegetarian.shtml
www.bbc.co.uk/food/vegetarian/
www.vegsoc.org/youth/index.html

Conversion chart

Ingredients for recipes can be measured in two different ways. Metric measurements use grams and millilitres. Imperial measurements use ounces and fluid ounces. This book uses metric measurements. The chart here shows you how to convert measurements from metric to imperial.

SOLIDS		LIQUIDS	
METRIC	IMPERIAL	METRIC	IMPERIAL
10 g	¼ oz	30 ml	1 fl oz
15 g	½ oz	50 ml	2 fl oz
25 g	1 oz	75 ml	2½ fl oz
50 g	1¾ oz	100 ml	3½ fl oz
75 g	2¾ oz	125 ml	4 fl oz
100 g	3½ oz	150 ml	5 fl oz
150 g	5 oz	300 ml	10 fl oz
250 g	9 oz	600 ml	20 fl oz
450 g	16 oz		

Healthy eating

This diagram shows which foods you should eat to stay healthy. Most of your food should come from the bottom of the pyramid. Eat some of the foods from the middle every day. Only eat a little of the foods from the top. Although the pyramid recommends meat, being a vegetarian does not mean you cannot eat healthily. Following a balanced vegetarian diet, which provides your body with enough **protein**, is very healthy indeed. Most of the foods we need to stay healthy are in the middle and bottom of this pyramid, which do not include any meat at all. Vegetarians must eat some foods from the top layer as well, such as **pulses**, nuts and milk.

Fats, oils, cakes and sweets

KEY
◻ Fat   ▼ Sugars

Milk, yoghurt and cheese

Meat, poultry, fish, pulses (beans and lentils), eggs and nuts

Vegetables

Fruit

Breads, cereal, rice and pasta

Glossary

bake cook something in the oven

beat mix ingredients together strongly, for example, egg yolks and whites

blend mix ingredients together in a blender or food processor

boil cook a liquid on the hob. Boiling liquid bubbles and steams strongly.

calcium mineral in foods, such as milk and cheese, that helps us have strong teeth and bones

chill put a dish into the fridge for a while

chop cut into pieces using a sharp knife

chutney a spicy sauce served with curries. Chutneys often contain chopped fruit and vegetables.

cover put a lid on a pan, or put foil or clingfilm over a dish

deep-fry cook in a deep pan of hot oil

drain remove liquid, usually by pouring something into a colander or sieve

dressing oil and vinegar sauce for salad

dry-fry fry in a pan without any oil

export to sell a product, such as fruit, to another country

fold mixing wet and dry ingredients by making cutting movements with a metal spoon

fondue set utensils used for melting cheese

fry cook something in oil in a pan

grate break something, such as cheese, into small pieces using a grater

grill cook under a grill

ground made into a fine powder

knead mix ingredients into a smooth dough for bread

mash crush a food until it is soft and pulpy

nutrient substance that provides nourishment

peel remove the skin of a fruit or vegetable

pitta bread flat, unrisen bread

preheat turn on the oven in advance, so that it is hot when you want to use it

protein a natural substance in food that our bodies need to stay healthy

pulse beans, peas or seeds from plants that often have pods

sift pass through a sieve

simmer cook liquid on the hob. Simmering liquid bubbles and steams gently.

slice cut into thin flat pieces

staple one of the most important foods in a person's diet is called a staple food

thawed no longer frozen

toast heat under a grill or in a toaster

vegan person who does not eat any food that has come from an animal, including milk and eggs

vegetarian food that does not contain meat. People who do not eat meat are called vegetarians.

vitamins natural chemicals in food that the body uses to stay healthy

whisk mix ingredients using a whisk

Index

Titles in the A World of Recipes series include:

Hardback   0431 117268

Hardback   0431 11725X

Hardback   0431 117284

Hardback   0431 117276

Hardback   0431 117306

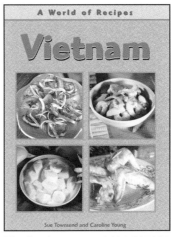

Hardback   0431 117292

Find out about the other titles in this series on our website www.heinemann.co.uk/library